# Exploring Materials

# Wood

## Abby Colich

Heinemann
LIBRARY
Chicago, Illinois

To contact Capstone Global Library please phone 800-747-4992, or visit our website www.capstonepub.com

Edited by Abby Colich, Daniel Nunn, and Catherine Veitch
Designed by Marcus Bell
Picture research by Tracy Cummins
Production by Victoria Fitzgerald
Originated by Capstone Global Library Ltd
Printed and bound in China by Leo Paper Products Ltd

17 16 15 14 13
10 9 8 7 6 5 4 3 2 1

**Library of Congress Cataloging-in-Publication Data**
Colich, Abby.
  Wood / Abby Colich.
      pages cm.—(Exploring materials)
  Includes bibliographical references and index.
  ISBN 978-1-4329-8020-7 (hb)—ISBN 978-1-4329-8028-3 (pb) 1.
Wood—Juvenile literature. I. Title.

TA419.C63 2014
620.1'2—dc23
                                            2012047525

**Acknowledgments**
The author and publisher are grateful to the following for permission to reproduce copyright material: Getty Images pp. 7 (© imagewerks), 11 (© John Telford); Shutterstock pp. 4 (© Little_Desire), 5 (© Mat Hayward), 6a (© parinyabinsuk), 6b (© Phiseksit), 6c (© czdast), 6d (© Xiebiyun), 8 (© MC_PP), 9 (© EpicStockMedia), 10 (© wdeon), 12 (© Hung Chung Chih), 13 (© senkaya), 14 (© thieury), 15, 23b (© Amy Walters), 16 (© Mike Flippo), 17 (© wavebreakmedia), 18 (© Ann Baldwin), 20 (© Maximus I), 21 (© iofoto), 22 (© Taina Sohlman, © Nenov Brothers Images), 23a (© EpicStockMedia); Superstock pp. 13 (© Cultura Limited), 19 (© Exactostock).

Cover photograph of girls painting birdhouses reproduced with permission of Superstock (© Corbis). Back cover photograph reproduced with permission of Shutterstock (© wdeon).

We would like to thank Valarie Akerson, Nancy Harris, Dee Reid, and Diana Bentley for their invaluable help in the preparation of this book.

Every effort has been made to contact copyright holders of any material reproduced in this book. Any omissions will be rectified in subsequent printings if notice is given to the publisher.

# Contents

# What Is Wood?

Wood is a material.

Materials are what things are made from.

Many things are made from wood.

Wood has many different uses.

# Where Does Wood Come From?

Wood comes from trees.

Some trees grow in forests.

People cut down trees to use
the wood.

Different trees give us different
types of wood.

# What Is Wood Like?

hard

soft

Wood can be hard or soft.

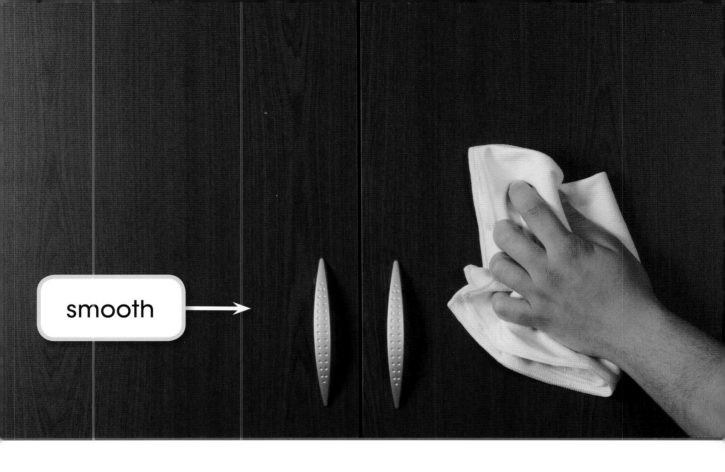

smooth

Wood can be smooth or rough.

Wood can be cut with a saw.

Wood can rot.

# How Do We Use Wood?

We use wood to build things.

We use wood to make instruments.

Wood can be used to make paper and cardboard.

Wood can be burned to keep
us warm.

Some toys and games are made from wood.

Some pencils are made from wood.

# Quiz

Which of these things are made from wood?

Answer on page 24.

# Picture Glossary

 **forest** large area covered with trees

 **rot** go to waste

# Index

The **logs (a)** and **building blocks (c)** are made from wood.

**Notes for Parents and Teachers**

**Before reading**

Ask children if they have heard the term "material" and what they think it means. Reinforce the concept of materials. Explain that all objects are made from different materials. A material is something that takes up space and can be used to make other things. Ask children to give examples of different materials. These may include metal, rock, and wood.

To get children interested in the topic, ask if they know what wood is. Identify any misconceptions they may have. Ask them to think about whether their ideas might change as the book is read.

**After reading**

• Check to see if any of the identified misconceptions have changed.
• Show the children examples of items made of wood, including clothespins, wooden spoons, and wooden blocks.
• Pass the wooden objects around. Ask the children to describe the properties of each object. Is the wood colored? Heavy or light? Ask them to name other items made from wood.